Common Core Lessons & Activities:

Declaration of Independence

By Carole Marsh
Published by Gallopade International, Inc.

Printed in the U.S.A. (Peachtree City, Georgia)

TABLE OF CONTENTS

G: Includes Graphic Organizer
GO: Graphic Organizer is also available
download at www.gallopade.com/
(numbers above correspond to the graphic

Early Independence

Read the text and answer the questions.

Many factors limited Great Britain's control over the colonies. From the beginning, the colonists enjoyed a good amount of independence from King George III. The vast distance of the Atlantic Ocean between Britain and the colonies made communication difficult. Britain could not control the colonies directly, so it gave the colonies charters to form their own governments. However, the French and Indian War caused Britain to seek to increase its control over the colonies.

The French and Indian War was a small part of a much larger war between Britain and France called The Seven Years' War. In the colonies, British and colonial forces defended the colonies against the French and France's Indian allies. Britain and the colonists won in 1763, but the war was very expensive for Britain.

The British government had to raise money to replenish funds used for the war. Since Britain defended the colonies in the war, they decided to tax the colonies. They passed several "acts" to raise taxes on colonial goods. The Sugar Act of 1764 and the Stamp Act of 1765 charged taxes on sugar and paper goods, and the Townshend Acts of 1767 taxed many imported goods. These new taxes angered colonists. To make matters worse, the colonists did not have a representative in Parliament. Many colonists argued that "taxation without representation" was unfair.

When colonists protested, King George III decided that the colonists had too much freedom to create laws. Thus, he removed the colonial governments. Many colonists saw King George III as a tyrant and began to suggest complete colonial independence.

1. Use a dictionary to define the following words.
   A. charter B. tax C. representation D. tyrant
2. What factors caused the colonists to have some independence from Britain before the French and Indian War?
3. Why did the British Government think it necessary to tax the colonies?
4. In your own words, explain "taxation without representation."
5. What event caused many colonists to see King George III as a tyrant?

MAIN IDEA ORGANIZER

Acts of Parliament

Identify the main Parliamentary acts and explain their significance to complete the graphic organizer.

ACTS OF PARLIAMENT

Intolerable Acts

Proclamation of 1763

Sugar Act of 1764

Townshend Acts

Currency Act

Stamp Act of 1765

Quartering Act

Sons of Liberty & The Boston Tea Party

Read the text and answer the questions.

The Sons of Liberty was an important group that supported independence from Great Britain. The first Sons of Liberty formed in Boston in 1765. They were a group of shopkeepers and artisans who were outraged by the Stamp Act. Their first protest in August 1765 provoked a violent mob attack on the house of Andrew Oliver, a Stamp Distributor for Massachusetts. By the end of the year, community leaders in every colony had formed a Sons of Liberty group. Their first and primary goal was to force Stamp Distributors to resign.

The Sons of Liberty often used symbols and political messages to provoke violence against British taxes and acts. However, their most effective messages were delivered in newsprint. Many of the members were printers or publishers. News of the Sons of Liberty's activities and beliefs was printed in nearly every colonial paper.

The most famous act of the Sons of Liberty occurred in Boston in December 1773. In protest of the Tea Act, the Boston Sons of Liberty dressed as Indians and boarded three East India Tea Company ships. Using tomahawks, they broke open the chests of tea and poured them into the Boston Harbor. The next morning, tea still floated on top of the water. Citizens and sailors manned small boats and sank the floating tea with paddles to prevent any tea from being recovered. British reaction was swift and forceful. In 1774, the British Parliament passed the Coercive Acts (Intolerable Acts), which closed Boston Harbor and brought the Massachusetts governments under British control.

1. What was the original purpose of the Sons of Liberty?
2. What methods did the Sons of Liberty use to oppose the British government? Which method was most effective?
3. Describe the Boston Tea Party from the point of view of a British royal governor. Include your opinion of the colonists and their actions.
4. Explain the relationship between the Boston Tea Party and the Coercive Acts. What sentence in the text supports your answer?

PRIMARY SOURCE ANALYSIS

The Boston Massacre

This engraving was produced by Paul Revere shortly after the Boston Massacre and printed for distribution in the colonies.

Look at the engraving and answer the questions.

Courtesy of Library of Congress

1. Describe what you see. What details do you notice first?
2. Identify the two groups of people shown.
3. What can you infer about the person who created this engraving? Cite evidence to support your conclusion.
4. Use a dictionary to define <u>massacre</u>. Does the word “massacre” accurately describe the image presented?
5. Write a response to this image from the perspective of a colonist. Read your response aloud and discuss.

COMPARISON OF PRIMARY SOURCES

"Paying the Excise-Man"

This political cartoon was published in 1774, entitled "Paying the Excise-Man." The text was written by Lord North, the Prime Minister of Great Britain, to King George III.

Look at the cartoon and read the text. Then answer the questions and complete the writing prompt.

The BOSTONIAN'S Paying the EXCISE-MAN, or TARRING & FEATHERING

Plate I.

Courtesy of Library of Congress

> The Americans have tarred and feathered your subjects, plundered your merchants, burnt your ships, denied all obedience to your laws and authority; yet so clement and so long forbearing has our conduct been that it is incumbent on us now to take a different course. Whatever may be the consequence, we must risk something; if we do not, all is over.
>
> — Prime Minister Lord North, defending the Coercive Acts

PART A: Look at the political cartoon and answer the questions.

1. Use a dictionary to define excise. Identify the "excise-man" in the cartoon.
2. What is happening in this cartoon? Use an online resource to describe the process of "tarring and feathering."
3. What can you infer about the cartoonist's opinion of British taxes?
4. What is the message of this political cartoon? What symbols or details does the cartoonist use to convey this message?

PART B: Read Lord North's quotation and answer the questions.

5. What is Lord North's opinion of American colonists? Support your conclusion with evidence from the text.
6. Use a dictionary to define clement. How do the British view their actions toward the colonists?
7. What is the tone of Lord North's message to King George III?
8. What words or phrases help you identify the tone?

PART C: Compare and contrast the cartoon and the text.

9. Explain how the cartoon and text differ in point of view.
10. Does Lord North's description of the Americans accurately describe the Americans in the cartoon "Paying the Excise-Man"? Explain why or why not.

Writing Prompt:

Imagine you are the British "Excise-Man" in the cartoon. Write a short response explaining your point of view. Include your reaction to being "tarred and feathered."

Loyalists, Neutralists, & Patriots

Read the text and fill in the graphic organizer by writing three opinion statements from the point of view of each colonist. An example has been provided.

The American Revolutionary War began in 1775, but that did not mean that all colonists were in agreement about declaring independence from Great Britain—they weren't! In fact, almost one-third of all colonists did not want independence at all!

Colonists who were loyal to King George III and against declaring independence were called loyalists. Loyalists had many reasons to remain faithful to Great Britain. Some loyalists wanted to keep British military protection. Other loyalists were still connected to Britain by family and history. Some colonists felt a strong sense of duty toward King George III. In fact, many colonists considered themselves British citizens instead of "American colonists."

Many colonists wished to remain neutral. Neutralists often valued independence but understood that Britain offered protection, government, and trade. They also were unsure about waging war.

Patriots, colonists who wanted independence, had many reasons to be unhappy with British rule. Many patriots were influenced by the writings of John Locke, who stated that men have the right to oppose unjust governments. The Sons of Liberty were the most famous group of patriots. They were not content with British taxes and longed for freedom from British rule. Patriots saw King George III as a tyrant who ruled unfairly, imposed unfair taxes, and used deadly violence against colonists in the Boston Massacre.

Loyalist	Neutralist	Patriot
1. King George III is our beloved king!	1.	1.
2.	2.	2.
3.	3.	3.

PRIMARY SOURCE ANALYSIS

"Join, or Die"

This political cartoon was first published in 1754 and reproduced in 1765 as a symbol supporting the American Revolution.

Analyze the cartoon and answer the questions.

Courtesy of Library of Congress

1. What is the main message of this cartoon?
2. Is the message stated directly or indirectly?
3. What symbols and words communicate that message?
4. Who is the intended audience of this cartoon?
5. Which colonies are represented?
6. Do you agree with the message presented? Explain.
7. From what political point of view is this cartoon depicted?
8. How does this picture relate to the Declaration of Independence?

The British Perspective

Read the text and answer the questions. Then complete the graphic organizer.

The colonists listed many complaints against the King, but King George III had a different point of view. For King George III, the Declaration of Independence was a clear sign of disrespect and defiance. Britain had recently defended the colonies during the French and Indian War. British Parliament thought a small tax on certain goods was a small price to pay for the protection of the British army. Britain left a standing army on guard in the colonies to protect the colonists from French and Indian attacks, and acts of Parliament were meant to help govern the colonies. Additionally, the British considered the colonies property of Great Britain.

The British side of key events, such as the Boston Massacre and the Boston Tea Party, tells a different side of history. British accounts of the Boston Massacre claimed that the massacre was an accident. They also accused the colonists of violently provoking and attacking British guards. When the Sons of Liberty threw British tea into Boston Harbor, British companies lost a large profit. The colonists' attempts at independence, including self-government and independent trade, angered the British government. The Declaration of Independence was final proof of colonial disrespect toward Great Britain and King George III.

1. Why did Great Britain leave a standing army in the colonies?
2. How did the Boston Tea Party affect the British?

Issue	British Point of View
Taxation	
Standing Army	
Boston Tea Party	
Boston Massacre	
Declaration of Independence	

CHRONOLOGICAL EVENTS

Path to the Declaration

Put the events in chronological order on the graphic organizer.

Second Continental Congress	French and Indian War	"Shot Heard Round the World"	The Townshend Acts	The Intolerable Acts
The Stamp Act	First Continental Congress	Boston Massacre	Boston Tea Party	The Proclamation Act

Pre-Declaration Events:

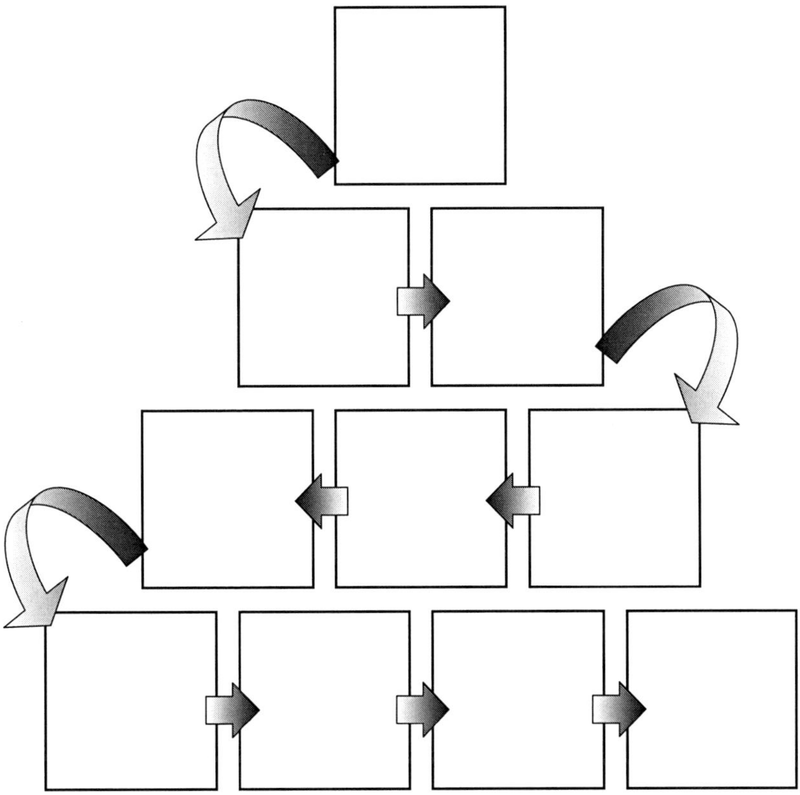

Mapping the Declaration – Summative Flowchart

Use the flowchart to summarize your knowledge of the Declaration of Independence. Identify pre-Declaration issues, elements of the Declaration, and results of declaring independence.

Pre-Declaration Issues

Issue

Issue

Issue

Issue

Issue

Elements of the Declaration

Purpose

Philosophy

Unalienable Rights

Results of the Declaration

Words of Declaration

Use a dictionary and other resources to complete the graphic organizer for each vocabulary word.

unalienable
declaration
independent
quartering
absolved

self-evident
endowed
intolerable
liberty
abolish

tyranny
loyalist
patriot
taxes
neutralist

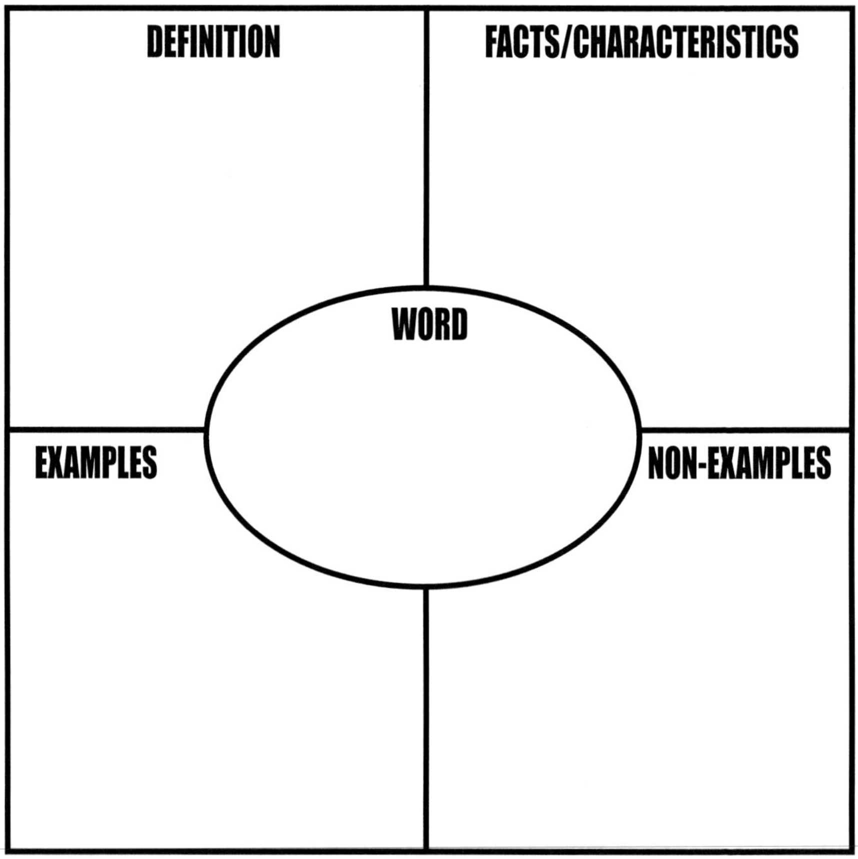

Authors of the Declaration

Read the text and answer the questions.

Thomas Jefferson was a well-known politician at the time of the American Revolution. He is often called the "Father of the Declaration of Independence" because he was responsible for writing the document. However, Thomas Jefferson did not write it alone.

Congress selected a "Committee of Five," including Benjamin Franklin, Roger Sherman, Richard R. Livingston, John Adams, and Thomas Jefferson, to produce the Declaration of Independence. Thomas Jefferson and the committee took many ideas from other writers and thinkers. One of these writers was George Mason.

George Mason was an important politician who wrote the Virginia Declaration of Rights. He was influenced by John Locke, who claimed all people should have certain rights. These rights are known as natural rights, which are basic rights that Mason believed no government should deny. Mason included the right to "enjoyment of life and liberty... and pursuing and obtaining happiness..." Thomas Jefferson used George Mason's Declaration of Rights as a model when writing the Declaration of Independence. Mason's work also had an important influence on another major American document, the Bill of Rights.

1. A. Define natural rights as it is used in the text.
   B. In your own words, give an example of a natural right.
2. Is "Father of the Declaration" a fair title for Thomas Jefferson? Why or why not?
3. How did George Mason's Virginia Declaration of Rights influence the Declaration of Independence?
4. Choose Benjamin Franklin, Roger Sherman, Richard R. Livingston, or John Adams. Use an online or classroom resource to find five important facts about that person. Share your facts with the class.

Drafting the Declaration

Read the text and answer the questions.

In 1774 the First Continental Congress met to petition King George III to repeal the Coercive Acts. The petition was ignored. After the "shot heard round the world" at Lexington and Concord on April 19, 1775, the Second Continental Congress met to make a second petition to the king. Again, the petition was ignored.

On June 7, 1776, the Congress passed the Lee Resolution to declare independence from Great Britain. Four days later, a committee of five, including Thomas Jefferson, John Adams, Benjamin Franklin, Robert R. Livingston, and Roger Sherman, was formed to write the Declaration of Independence.

Together, the committee created a general outline. Jefferson was assigned the task of writing the first draft. When Jefferson finished writing, the other four men made changes. Jefferson included the changes in a second draft, and the declaration was presented to Congress on June 28, 1776. Congress made changes to the Declaration from July 1 to July 4, declaring independence on July 2, and adopting the declaration of Independence on July 4. The same committee of five produced a final "fair copy" on the evening of July 4. It was then printed on July 5 and read aloud in public areas.

The handwritten copy that was signed by Congress is dated July 4, 1776. The Declaration was printed on July 5, but the United States still celebrates Independence Day on July 4. However, many signers were not present at the time, and several did not sign until August 2, 1776.

1. What was the purpose of petitions sent to King George III by the First and Second Continental Congresses?
2. Use the text to make a list of the steps involved in creating the Declaration of Independence in the order they occurred.
3. Do you think creating the Declaration of Independence was a simple process? Explain why or why not.
4. Why does the U.S. celebrate Independence Day on July 4?

Structure of the Declaration

Read the text and answer the questions.

The Declaration of Independence is a statement against British control on trade, government, and political representation. In fact, it says that the colonies are free from Parliament and King George III. Overall, the Declaration explains and justifies the colonists' independence and gives a straightforward list of reasons why the colonies separated from Great Britain.

The first section of the Declaration, called the Preamble, states that the American people, when necessary, have the right to declare independence. The second section explains the ideas behind the Declaration. According to the Declaration, everyone has "certain unalienable rights," including "Life, Liberty, and the pursuit of Happiness." It says that the purpose of government is to protect those natural rights. In addition, people can change or oppose their government if those unalienable rights are in danger.

The third section is a long list of the colonists' complaints against King George III, including taxation and unfair trials. The fourth section claims that the colonists tried to find solutions and make peace. The fifth section restates the colonists' determination to defend their independence and rights. The last section is a list of signers representing all 13 colonies. Congressional delegates signed the Declaration to show the commitment of the colonies to protecting independence from Great Britain.

1. What is the purpose of the Declaration of Independence?
2. Describe the five main parts of the Declaration of Independence, not including the signers.
3. From the text, what is the key purpose of a government?
4. According to the Declaration, when do people have the right to oppose an oppressive government?
5. Explain the purpose of the fourth section. Why might the colonists have included it?
6. If you were a congressional delegate in 1776, would you have signed the Declaration of Independence? Why or why not?

Key Philosophy

Read the text and answer the questions.

The Declaration of Independence clearly states the colonists' purpose and reasoning for separating from the British monarchy. However, the ideas and philosophy behind the Declaration are not original to America. Thomas Jefferson admitted that the ideas were borrowed from other sources, including from John Locke, an English philosopher.

The Declaration includes several key ideas from John Locke's *Two Treatises of Government*. Locke thought that government should protect people's rights. Locke believed that government should be given power by the people—government should not take power. This idea would later be called popular sovereignty. Locke also thought that people could change any government that threatens the people's unalienable rights. Those natural rights, especially for Locke, included the right to "life, health, liberty, or possessions" (Locke). Jefferson then changed the statement to "Life, Liberty, and the pursuit of Happiness" (Declaration of Independence).

Locke's *Two Treatises of Government* expressed the idea that all men are free, equal, and allowed to protect their "unalienable Rights." Therefore, if men are free, they should not be forced to live under a tyrant. The drafters of the Declaration strongly claimed that British acts were denying them their unalienable rights.

1. Make a list of Locke's beliefs and summarize them in your own words.
2. How did Locke's *Two Treatises of Government* influence the Declaration of Independence?
3. Use the text to define popular sovereignty. How did the colonists use this concept to argue for independence from King George III?
4. According to John Locke's philosophy, when is it necessary to change one's government?
5. Use a Venn diagram to compare and contrast the unalienable rights according to John Locke's writing and the Declaration of Independence.

Key Declaration Excerpts

Rewrite each excerpt to complete the chart. Use the completed chart to answer the questions.

Declaration Excerpts:	Rewrite in your own words:
"We hold these truths to be self-evident, that all men are created equal, that they are endowed by their Creator with certain unalienable Rights…"	
"That whenever any Form of Government becomes destructive of these ends, it is the Right of the People to alter or to abolish it, and to institute new Government..."	
"A Prince whose character is thus marked by every act which may define a Tyrant and is unfit to be the ruler of a free people..."	

1. Look up the definition of the following words and write a synonym for each.
   A. self-evident B. endowed C. abolish D. tyrant
2. What truths are considered "self-evident" according to the first excerpt?
3. What government is being described in the second excerpt?
4. What can you infer about the colonists' opinion of King George III from the third excerpt?

List of Complaints

The Declaration of Independence was a formal announcement to King George III that the colonists were separating from Great Britain. The colonists included a list of 27 complaints against King George III to make clear the reasons for separation.

Ten of the colonists' major complaints are listed below. Read each complaint and use the chart to rewrite each complaint from the perspective of a colonist. Two examples have been given. Use a dictionary to look up unfamiliar words. Then answer the questions.

1. For Quartering large bodies of armed troops among us
2. He has obstructed the Administration of Justice, by refusing his Assent to Laws for establishing Judiciary powers
3. For cutting off our Trade with all parts of the world
4. For depriving us in many cases, of the benefits of Trial by Jury
5. For transporting us beyond Seas to be tried for pretended offenses
6. For taking away our Charters, abolishing our most valuable Laws, and altering fundamentally the Forms of our Government
7. He has plundered our seas, ravaged our Coasts, burnt our towns, and destroyed the lives of our people
8. He has dissolved Representative Houses repeatedly, for opposing with manly firmness his invasions on the rights of the people
9. He has forbidden his Governors to pass Laws of immediate and pressing importance... till his Assent should be obtained; and when so suspended, he has utterly neglected to attend to them
10. He has abdicated Government here, by declaring us out of his Protection and waging War against us

---

1. Circle any words and phrases generally having a negative connotation.
2. What can you infer about the colonists' opinion of King George III? What words and phrases support your conclusion?

#	What each complaint means to me
1.	The King put BRITISH soldiers in OUR homes!
2.	There is no justice under the King! He has dissolved our laws and courts.
3.	
4.	
5.	
6.	
7.	
8.	
9.	
10.	

Created Equal?

Read the text and answer the questions in paragraph form.

The Declaration of Independence states, "all men are created equal." It also claims that all men are given certain unalienable rights. However, in early American history, black men and women were not equal and had few rights. Thomas Jefferson himself owned approximately 200 slaves, and slavery was an important form of labor in the agricultural south until 1865.

Jefferson's first draft of the Declaration included a paragraph against slavery. He claimed that King George III had promoted the slave trade in America. In fact, at the outbreak of the American Revolution, Great Britain offered freedom to all slaves who would fight with the British against the colonies. Both southern and northern slaveholders wanted the paragraph against slavery removed. Slavery was a cheap form of labor for the colonies. When Congress reviewed the first draft on July 1, 1776, the section against slavery was removed.

Although the Declaration of Independence celebrates human rights and freedom, slavery existed in America until 1865. For approximately a century after the Declaration of Independence, African American men and women were denied their "unalienable Rights."

1. Why did the colonies want Thomas Jefferson to remove the paragraph about slavery?
2. Explain how Great Britain used slavery against the colonies.
3. In a well-organized speech, share your response to the question "If all men are created equal, why did slavery exist?"
4. In American history, women did not receive the right to vote until 1920. Is it possible that Thomas Jefferson meant "all MEN are created equal," while excluding women? Discuss your thoughts as a class.
5. Predict what might have happened if the Declaration of Independence specifically outlawed slavery in the United States.

Influence of the Declaration

Read the text and answer the questions.

The Declaration of Independence has had a lasting influence in U.S. history. In many cases, the Declaration of Independence has been used to support civil and human rights in the United States. Abolitionists, such as Frederick Douglass, used the Declaration to argue that slavery is unjust and that "all men are created equal." Elizabeth Cady Stanton and other supporters of women's equality used the Declaration of Independence to write their *Declaration of Sentiments*. Additionally, the Confederacy used the Declaration as a model for declaring secession from the Union.

The U.S. Declaration of Independence has also been influential in the history of other countries. After the U.S won its independence from Great Britain, other countries saw opportunity to claim their unalienable rights. Most notably, the leaders of the French Revolution in 1789 admired the colonists' struggle against an oppressive British government. The French *Declarations of the Rights of Man and of the Citizen* contains similar language and content to the Declaration of Independence. Additionally, the U.S. Declaration provided an example for officially declaring a new government. Several countries that declared independence, including Haiti, Venezuela, and Vietnam, modeled their declarations of independence after the U.S. Declaration.

1. What is the main idea of the text?
2. How is the main idea developed and supported?
3. Write an appropriate subtitle for each paragraph.
4. List three ways the Declaration of Independence affected United States history.
5. According to the text, what qualities of the U.S. Declaration influenced the French Revolution?
6. Why did countries like Haiti and Venezuela model their declarations after the U.S. Declaration of Independence?

Correlations to Common Core State Standards

For your convenience, correlations are listed page-by-page and for the entire book!

This book is correlated to the Common Core State Standards for English Language Arts grades 3-8, and to Common Core State Standards for Literacy in History, Science, & Technological Subjects grades 6-8.

Correlations are highlighted in gray.

PAGE #	READING *Includes:* RI: Reading Informational Text RH: Reading History	WRITING *Includes:* W: Writing WHST: Writing History, Science, & Technology	LANGUAGE *Includes:* L: Language LF: Language Foundational Skills	SPEAKING & LISTENING *Includes:* SL: Speaking & Listening
2	RI RH . **1** **2** 3 **4** 5 6 7 8 9 **10**	W WHST . 1 2 3 4 5 6 7 8 9 10	L LF . 1 2 3 **4** 5 **6**	SL . 1 2 3 4 5 6
3	RI RH . **1** **2** 3 4 5 6 7 8 9 **10**	W WHST . 1 2 3 4 5 6 7 8 9 10	L LF . 1 2 3 4 5 6	SL . 1 2 3 4 5 6
4	RI RH . **1** **2** **3** 4 5 6 7 8 9 **10**	W WHST . **1** 2 **3** **4** 5 6 7 8 9 **10**	L LF . 1 2 3 4 5 6	SL . 1 2 3 4 5 6
5	RI RH 1 2 3 **4** 5 6 **7** 8 **9** **10**	W WHST 1 2 **3** **4** 5 6 7 8 9 **10**	L LF 1 2 3 **4** 5 **6**	SL **1** 2 3 **4** 5 **6**
6-7	RI RH . **1** **2** 3 **4** **5** 6 **7** **8** **9** **10**	W WHST . **1** 2 **3** **4** 5 6 **7** **8** **9** **10**	L LF . 1 2 3 **4** 5 **6**	SL . 1 2 3 4 5 6
8	RI RH . **1** 2 3 4 5 6 7 8 9 **10**	W WHST . 1 2 3 4 5 6 7 8 9 10	L LF . 1 2 3 4 5 6	SL . 1 2 3 4 5 6
9	RI RH . 1 2 3 4 5 **6** **7** 8 9 **10**	W WHST . 1 2 3 4 5 6 7 8 9 10	L LF . 1 2 3 4 5 6	SL . 1 2 3 4 5 6
10	RI RH **1** **2** 3 4 5 6 7 8 9 **10**	W WHST 1 2 3 4 5 6 7 8 9 10	L LF 1 2 3 4 5 6	SL 1 2 3 4 5 6
11	RI RH . 1 2 3 4 **5** 6 7 8 9 **10**	W WHST . 1 2 3 4 5 6 7 8 9 10	L LF . 1 2 3 4 5 6	SL . 1 2 3 4 5 6
12-13	RI RH . 1 2 3 4 **5** 6 7 8 **9** **10**	W WHST . 1 2 3 4 5 6 7 **8** **9** **10**	L LF . 1 2 3 4 5 6	SL . 1 2 3 4 5 6
14	RI RH . 1 2 3 **4** 5 6 7 8 9 **10**	W WHST . 1 2 3 4 5 6 7 **8** 9 **10**	L LF . 1 2 3 **4** 5 **6**	SL . 1 2 3 4 5 6
15	RI RH . **1** **2** 3 **4** 5 6 7 8 9 **10**	W WHST . 1 2 3 4 5 6 **7** **8** **9** **10**	L LF . 1 2 3 **4** 5 **6**	SL . 1 2 3 4 5 6
16	RI RH . **1** **2** 3 4 **5** 6 7 8 9 **10**	W WHST . 1 2 3 4 5 6 7 8 9 10	L LF . 1 2 3 4 5 6	SL . 1 2 3 4 5 6
17	RI RH . **1** **2** 3 4 5 6 7 8 9 **10**	W WHST . 1 **2** 3 **4** 5 6 7 8 9 **10**	L LF . 1 2 3 4 5 6	SL . 1 2 3 4 5 6
18	RI RH . **1** **2** 3 **4** **5** 6 7 8 9 **10**	W WHST . 1 **2** 3 **4** 5 6 7 8 9 **10**	L LF . 1 2 3 **4** 5 **6**	SL . 1 2 3 4 5 6
19	RI RH . **1** 2 3 **4** 5 6 7 8 9 **10**	W WHST . 1 2 3 4 5 6 7 8 9 10	L LF . 1 2 3 **4** **5** **6**	SL . 1 2 3 4 5 6
20-21	RI RH . **1** **2** 3 **4** 5 6 7 8 9 **10**	W WHST . 1 2 3 4 5 6 7 8 9 10	L LF . 1 2 3 **4** 5 **6**	SL . 1 2 3 4 5 6
22	RI RH . **1** **2** 3 **4** 5 6 7 8 9 **10**	W WHST . **1** **2** **3** **4** **5** **6** 7 8 9 **10**	L LF . 1 2 3 **4** 5 **6**	SL . **1** 2 3 **4** 5 **6**
23	RI RH . 1 **2** 3 4 5 6 7 8 9 **10**	W WHST . 1 2 3 4 5 6 7 8 9 10	L LF . 1 2 3 4 5 6	SL . 1 2 3 4 5 6
COMPLETE BOOK	RI RH . **1** **2** **3** **4** **5** **6** **7** **8** **9** **10**	W WHST . **1** **2** **3** **4** **5** **6** **7** **8** **9** **10**	L LF . 1 2 3 **4** **5** **6**	SL . **1** 2 3 **4** 5 **6**

For the complete Common Core standard identifier, combine your grade + "." + letter code above + "." + number code above.

In addition to the correlations indicated here, the activities may be adapted or expanded to align to additional standards and to meet the diverse needs of your unique students!